Unflinchingly honest and intimate, Elfick and Head find the words to express the inexpressible: not only the humiliating indignities that accompany human decline and death and the ambivalent feelings evoked by intimacy, but the experience of caring for, parting from and staying with the dying.

Chaplains or professionals whose roles are to minister to the suffering of the seriously ill and dying do not usually acknowledge the limits of their profession or their own vulnerabilities. There were so many lines I wanted to quote: "Perhaps a 'hospice' poem is where I put the stuff I'm not allowed to say/or think. Therapy without conjunctions" being the simplest. This amazing volume refuses to accept reductionist answers to the inexplicable questions of life and death. Accessible, riveting, unsentimental, the shocks of recognition in these terse poems move the reader from tears, to laughter, to stunning silence as we witness the profound power in this caring for, parting from and staying with the dying. Required reading for all experienced or novice healthcare professionals concerned with end of life care.

Sandra Bertman

Sandra Bertman, PhD, is Research Professor of Palliative Care at Boston University Graduate School of Social Work. Formerly Professor of Humanities in Medicine, she pioneered the use of the arts, humanities and expressive therapies to advance the knowledge of the psychology of loss, suffering, and spirituality at the University of Massachusetts Medical and Graduate Schools of Nursing, where she founded the program of Medical Humanities and the Arts in Health Care. Her publications include the classic handbooks *Facing Death: Images, Insights and Interventions*, and *Grief and the Healing Arts: Creativity as Therapy*.

This is a fine collection: honest, uncompromising, uncomfortable, and yet ultimately deeply comforting. Each poet approaches the subject in an array of styles and voices, yet with an authenticity of experience which unifies the book. I think it will give tremendous support to all who read it.

The shape of the collection is very strong. Cynthia Fuller has done a wonderful job, establishing the two poets' individual voices at the outset, then moving through illness and care, pain and comfort, death, loss and grieving, towards a positive end, which celebrates the dead, affirms poetry's power to immortalise, and sets death within the wider context of Christian belief and the earth's natural cycles, eternal and redemptive.

Cynthia has also written an excellent introduction. I agree with everything she says: about the range, honesty and compassion each poet displays; about the way their poetry focuses on the transformations which extreme situations bring into being; and about the way in which their words stretch and rise to this challenge. Above all, I agree with what she says about the comfort and consolation which this collection will give.

I love Hilary Elfick's development of David Head's line, "Prayer is absolute attention to what is the case" (from 'Attention') in her line "What is grieving, but attending to the fact that you have gone?" ('Elegy for a Tutor'). Whether or not this is a deliberate connection, it seems so, and works beautifully to unify the collection. Hence, of course, the title.

So – fine work from each of them: intimate, uncomfortable, loving and true. There is much human experience in this collection, a depth of loss and despair, and yet hope is always present. There is something for everyone, at every stage. *Attending to the Fact* offers a helping hand, that most valuable of comforts: a reminder that, although we each travel the road on our own, none of us is alone on our journey.

Katrina Porteous

Katrina Porteous was Writer-in-Residence at the 2002 Aldeburgh Poetry Festival and was awarded an Arts Foundation Fellowship in poetry for 2003. Her work is published by Bloodaxe.

Attending to the Fact – Staying with Dying

Hilary Elfick and David Head

Edited by Cynthia Fuller

Jessica Kingsley Publishers
London and New York

Cover by David Head, from a painting entitled 'The Look', after Primaticcio.

First published in the United Kingdom in 2004
by Jessica Kingsley Publishers Ltd
116 Pentonville Road
London N1 9JB, England
and
29 West 35th Street, 10th fl.
New York, NY 10001-2299, USA

www.jkp.com

Library of Congress Cataloging in Publication Data
Elfick, Hilary.
Attending to the fact : staying with dying / poems by Hilary Elfick and David Head ; edited by Cynthia Fuller ; forewords by Andrew Hoy, Sandra Bertman, and Katrina Porteous.
p. cm.
Includes index.
ISBN 1-84310-247-1 (pbk.)
1. Hospices (Terminal care)--Poetry. 2. Terminally ill--Poetry. 3. Hospice care--Poetry. 4. Death--Poetry. I. Head, David, 1955- II. Fuller, Cynthia, 1948- III. Title.
PR6055.L35A95 2004
821'.9208--dc22

2004002662

British Library Cataloguing in Publication Data
A CIP catalogue record for this book is available from the British Library

ISBN 1 84310 247 1

Printed and Bound in Great Britain by
Athenaeum Press, Gateshead, Tyne and Wear

Foreword

Care for the dying is as old as time, although palliative medicine is one of the youngest of specialities. This collection of poems by Hilary Elfick and David Head is subtitled *Staying with Dying*. In years to come, the last third of the twentieth century will be recognised as the time when not only the caring professions but also society in general rediscovered the necessity for palliative care. We can acknowledge the need for staying with the dying in the same way that we must nurture and care for the new-born.

The bio-medical revolution of the last two hundred years has brought huge benefits, but there is sometimes a danger that the art of caring has been overshadowed by technological advance. This anthology redresses that balance. These poems show the reader the human side of care. There is humour, sadness, joy and pain here. There is almost unbearable pathos and there is existential perplexity. These poems teach truths about hospice philosophy which would otherwise go without notice. The poems ring true. They must be essential reading for professional carers as well as for patients and families.

Dr Andrew Hoy
Chairman of the Association for Palliative Medicine of Great Britain and Ireland

in memory of two men
who gave us spiritual direction

Donald Nicholl
and
Simon Phipps

Contents

Introduction

This collection brings together two distinct voices, Hilary Elfick, an experienced poet who has published five collections, and David Head whose involvement in poetry is more recent. Their shared experience is in their work with hospices, David Head in the capacity of chaplain, and Hilary Elfick as a member of council, bringing her educational and creative writing skills into this area. The poems provide a moving and intense expression of this work, and together take the reader into the daily life of the hospice and beyond.

Editing a collection is always exciting, but there is also the moment of doubt or anxiety, just in case editor and poems don't "get on". As I read through the work for the first time I became completely absorbed in the stories, the characters and the emotions. I found the honesty, the uncompromising look at pain and loss, and the compassion of the work compelling. Looking at the work as poetry, I found a range of approach. There are poems that are confident in their use of regular metre and fixed forms, and poems that make bold experiments with layout and pattern. The problem then became how to select from this rich and varied material.

I only know the two poets from their work. I formed some impressions — both hone in on precisely observed details of the natural world, both are comfortable with different voices and tones, and can write in an intimate way that draws the reader into the personal world very immediately. I wanted to let each poet "speak" in the opening pages of the collection so that the reader has a sense of meeting them as individuals and sees something of their particular perspectives.

Thereafter I felt a shape emerging. The collection moves through different aspects of illness and care, pain and comfort, death, loss and grieving, taking a range of perspectives which open up the experiences and allow the reader to meditate and explore. The poems grouped themselves thematically but I was also looking for poems that worked as poems. Because the subject matter is very emotive, very moving, I felt that the poems had to rise to that in their technical sureness. I was looking for sharpness in language and skilful use of sound; interesting line breaks and stanza patterns. I wanted the collection to demonstrate variety in the register of language and in the effects created by rhythm and music. I wanted it to grab the reader by its poetry. Sometimes I rejected a poem which told a vivid story if the poetry of the telling did not feel "tight" or focused enough.

A group of poems focuses upon the individual's experience of illness. Sometimes the poems observe, sometimes they are the voice of the patient. Each poem has a story, conveys the sense of a complex life. I was struck by the way the poetry crystallises the transformations brought about by extreme situations, transformations both physical and psychological. The voices speak directly to the reader who will find echoes of experience, will recognise the emotions. Patients, families and carers are all represented. There is no avoidance of the difficult; the same precise attention is given to bodily changes as to the beauty of trees, colours, and flowers. What I particularly liked was the inclusiveness. The patients whose stories are told are not "they" but "we". The illness, the tragedies, the loss are expressed as part of all our experience, poets and readers too. Poems about individual patients are interspersed with poems exploring connecting themes in the poets' lives, bringing out the commonality of suffering. Many of these poems will stay with me – 'Billy is my child' and 'This woman should have been my mother' have left a lasting impression, and 'Your Father Phoned' and 'Euphemisms' I have gone back to several times.

There are poems that reflect upon the experience of working in the hospice. I was struck by David Head's lines, "My function is to ease the passage, / but of whom to what I am not sure" ('The Hospice Chaplain's Royal Road') and "We take talk, dig dark holes in the soul / for light and time to shine through" ('Visitor Hour'). The reader goes with the poet from bedside to bedside, is taken into intimate situations and allowed to share the different kinds of emotions felt. The openness of the voice and the sense of connection with each person come across vividly, and each poem is particular in its lay out and shape. There is no glossing over complex feelings or doubts. The honesty of these poems will give support to the families of patients and to others working in the field.

Reading through the collection I was made aware of a community where each member is engaged in a difficult journey. Relationships are under stress, and at their strongest. The poems encompass death and grieving, responding to the themes in many different ways. There is the poignant music of 'Breaking the Thread', which contrasts with the starker tone of 'Keeping Time'. Each reader will take a particular path through these poems, discovering that one tone will be right at one stage, another at a later stage. The poems have that authenticity of experience, which both moves us, and lets us in to contemplate our own losses.

The collection moves through death, loss and bereavement, the strong elegiac poems in the final pages demonstrating poetry's power to celebrate and immortalise the dead. Throughout the journey the poems keep the natural world in view, its seasons and cycles. We share the acuteness of loss yet hope is never completely absent – "One anachronistic spear of green / Has cheeked its way through the shroud." ('Winter'). There is no minimising of pain but it is set in the context of a world where memory slips into eternity, where all experience has its place, and we can "look up to / find my Lord still here across the dappled shade" ('Courtyard at Emmaus').

Cynthia Fuller

Cynthia Fuller is involved in research into poetry and health at Newcastle University. She is a poet who teaches literature and creative writing in Adult and Higher Education, running writing workshops for many different groups including schools and colleges and adult groups in the community as well as hospices. For twelve years she was a poetry editor for the magazine *Writing Women*.

In addition to her current research, she is teaching creative writing courses for Leeds University in Middlesbrough, and literature for the Open University. She has had three books of poems published by Flambard Press – *Moving Towards Light* (1992); *Instructions for the Desert* (1996); *Only a Small Boat* (2001) and is working on her next collection.

Questions

So why are you not telling me about the rest?
Because it's not your story and not your fault.

Why have you stopped eating?
It is the fast before the wake, and before the festival.

Are the decisions hard?
The decision for or against truth is the only life or death decision.

Are there dragons?
Yes.

Are you safe?
I have learnt it is not possible to walk out of the circle of God.

Is it dark?
I kneel in shadows at the day's ending.

Are you cold?
The hands that hold me are warm.

Can you sleep?
I have woken with a start into the memory of loving.

Do you keep a candle lit for me?
The light burns of itself. I do not know who fuels it.

Need I keep a night watch for you?
No. Go your own journey. I shall still be there in the morning.

Hilary Elfick

Iles Lavezzi

A lizard lay like you
Panting on a rock
Scurrying for shade
And darting out again

We were companionable
On the granite headstones
The seabirds cried around us
Dry lichens moved lightly

In the quivering breeze
Water lapped. Your ghost
The lizard and the seabirds
The slowly yellow flowering

Outcrop and the carved letters
Of passionate outpouring
A mother for her son
Strummed like the cicadas in the shimmering heat

Hilary Elfick

The hill

The hill I am over is covered in clover
and orchids and kids and more kids
flying kites, running, wheeling,
shouting like starlings, the darlings,
and blue-sky clouds whooshing away
to the west and the best of the day
is to come and the sun is high as a kite
and the elms on the plain cast small shadows,
and swallows encircle me, swooping
and rolling, and golden-haired girls
leap barefoot on sleek turf, and flutes
play at larks, and bearded men dance
with the fallow deer fording the stream,
and the lichen on rocks stop to examine
the host they slowly creep over, the mole
leaves his mounds in a curve and the ground
is as holy as taking off socks, shoes, galoshes
can make it, and the beckoning warmth
of grey haze below here keeps the road
indistinct I must follow.

Or so I tell myself.

David Head

Flat

the only place I want to be
is with my bum at waterlevel in a clinker-built dinghy
sailing end to end of the tidal lagoon
full at the flood
marsh growth mere wisps of sea-lavender above a flat surface
terns tridents that plunge back into the sea
sleep-sleep-sleep of wavelets at the forefoot
battened leech curved white against startling blue
broad dazzle-track towards the sun
hazy elongated slice of farmland and village
      and the helm over
dunes worn away with wind and footprints
pebbles studding the smoothed swell of shoreline at the point
one remaining brick wall of the house built on sand
boats and boards pulled up flapping on the beach
hardy picnickers near the ferry landing
the low stretch of the island that covers at springs
spiny crushed velvet of marram
the channel through to the next harbour
      and the helm over
duck slide sit on the eastward tack
      again and again side to side of this flatness
like the shuttle of amnesia's loom making something insubstantial

David Head

Meg

She used to keep such a pretty house
Geraniums well-watered in the porch
Kitchen spotless, bathroom sweet
A shine in the paintwork and her face

She can't reach so high any more
Her balance is unreliable.
The kids that run past her door
Never knew her when she was young.
She spills things down her frock
And dribbles in her stockings
When the warnings come too late.
She knows. That makes it worse.
That bit of chicken she had
Was that today? And tomorrow
Her nephew will take her away.

There will be no memories
In the room he has found for her.
She is not required to pack them.

Hilary Elfick

Paying for it

Each day takes ninety pounds from my estate.
This nursing home's expensive in my eyes.
My children can't look after me. I wait

for death to take my body, liberate
the little stash I slaved to realise;
each day takes ninety pounds from my estate.

The nurse is foreign or the shifts rotate.
She smoothes the bed and smothers me with lies.
My children can't look after me. I wait

and watch the calendar with each new date
undo my life in leaps, reduce its size;
each day takes ninety pounds from my estate.

So they'd inherit more, I'd moderate
my needs, and now I need a compromise
my children can't look after me. I wait

in hope clots stop me, or I suffocate,
or choke on food; just death in any guise.
My children can't look after me. I wait.
Each day takes ninety pounds from my estate.

David Head

Maxillo-facial

Her face shortens.
The dressings grow.
It is inexorable,
    if slow.

The hole widens
where bone once was.
Why is her beauty attacked?
    Because.

She does not fret,
does not complain,
does not behave like someone
    in pain.

She has a large
lip-swollen smile.
The creeping damage can't swamp
    her style.

Her spoken words
I understand
but she writes long messages
    by hand

down on paper,
feelings, love, fears,
sheets of three-dimensional
    ideas

concern and care
in blue on white.
She goes at it all day and
all night.

The fact she's ill
meant that we met.
Don't wish this on anyone.
And yet.

Such bravery,
courage, wit, grace.
There's immense dignity in
her face.

Those who meet her
can't help seeing
this holed body holds a whole
being.

David Head

Tear-tracks

The lines through the pancake
  on your lower cheek
snake like adjacent rivers
  in the Colorado dust.
The pale face between the ridges
  of braved-on pink
is autumn-watercourse dry,
  vacant, and sinuous.

The Grand Canyon is striated,
  a mile deep chasm,
gouged by its own eternity
  of fret, grinding out
a pre-ordained swerving track
  through the plain with
the heavy leavings of far
  thunderstorms.

Your words flow, and the damage
  on your pretty face
displays the strength and weakness
  of your make-up.
The patch of glossy blusher
  is impregnable.
Below meanders the geology
  of your grief.

David Head

Mary

4.4.74

The seepage had gone on all night
but still I thought you were intact.

When morning came and they brought the bedpan
a warm lump slid between my thighs.

Stilled by deepest silence
I cramped my buttocks
fearing to squeeze excrement
over your quiet and naked fragility.

The nurse who came briskly to collect
startled, peered where I had feared to look.
"I think you just lost your baby.
Wait while I fetch Sister."

Head on the pillow, dry-eyed,
back arched to fit
the warming metal of the pan.

"Lift yourself" said Sister. "Yes."
They took away the cooling contents.

Lifetime later, quiet she sat by my bed.
"Your cord broke.
I christened her. That's why
I went so quickly."
"What name?"
"Mary, I think" she said, surprised.
"Does it matter?
She was perfect down to her tiny fingernails.
I shall use her to teach the nurses."

"I still need the bedpan" I said.

Hilary Elfick

Influence of the moon

Her head flailed, whipped like wipers
failing to clear a frosted windscreen.
She groaned, howled, held the swollen stomach
beyond her puddled breasts.

Hands, words, the injection,
did not calm her. Her eyes closed,
she strained upwards as if called,
threshed again, pawed at her pain.

A hormone-born fuzz of brown down crept
from hairline to eyebrows. Definite, feminine, fur
crowded the cheeks, upper lip, and dimpled chaps
of her drug-rounded face.

Her metamorphosis hangs
in my dark mind. Above the icy road
of my way home, I too
feel the pull of the full moon.

David Head

Writing out the angst

for Sue Joslin

If you tell me
I must shift my shit
you must not then complain
if I write about excrement.

And if I am as constipated
as you, my wise one, think
then you see I may need
a lot of paper.

Only tell me
when your eyes are smarting
that it is more than the smell
that moves you.

Hilary Elfick

Lifelong

Lifelong I have believed
in the death penalty. An eye for an eye.
They deserve it. Let them swing.

And now me. I've done nothing.
Condemned and innocent; time ticks away.
There's no way you can tell me this is fair.

The chaplain came. I don't know why.
It's traditional. We had nothing to say.
He was no comfort. He didn't pray.

At least he didn't ask me to confess.
I've done nothing. What's the point of being good.
Bugger it. Bugger God.

How long have I got? A week? A day?
At least there's no date set, I can't count down
to a judicially fixed day at dawn.

I can't say each passed second is a second less.
It feels like one more, something spare.
Extending the gap. But it will come.

Yes, big D, I know you're there.
Somewhere, just around the corner, bunkum.
I am not ready. I want more time.

I want a stay of execution.
The longer the better. I can wait.
Let the guilty die. Not me. Not who I am.

Since I knew, I've been hanging on.
I mean to hang longer than any dead felon
left as an example in the air.

Come again, chaplain, and do no harm.
Like a last breakfast. Useless but on a plate.
Listen if you want. Just don't press.

I have done nothing. I am doing nothing.
When big D comes, I shall do nothing.
I'm hanging, hanging around for nothing.

When nothing happens, I shall be relieved.

David Head

Writing out the angst – 2

To find out how I am
will you pick over my entrails
or will it be enough
to cast a discriminating eye
over my bedpan?

Is it only undigested mass
which has made me so to swell
or have I by some accident
and time's long secret alchemy
compressed a diamond
from all those dead, primaeval leaves?

Is it possible that all that stored waste
held to the light in your wise hands
might astonish and sparkle like Joseph's coat?

Or shall we regretfully discard
and jettison all we find here,
discovering, after all,
that there was nothing worth preserving?

Hilary Elfick

Hot weather

Now I've decided to go, I no longer want to die.
Dust on each bonnet in the car park
reminds me of teddy bear fur,
the litter of cherry petals of successful confetti,
the partial greening of trees of lace brassieres,
traffic of sixty-four-foot stops on a cathedral organ,
streetlamps of the repeal of the death sentence.

It's leaving that liberates. Even the prosaic.
Papers kept in case can scrumple,
books receive overblown dedications and disperse,
caseloads be reassigned,
the year-planner stripped of stars and bars beyond the line.

It can't be merely Spring.
The building slips its glad-rags on to wave goodbye.
Cobwebs hang in the eaves like handkerchiefs,
canteen food is colourful as bunting,
doors open with the creak of musical greeting cards,
blankets in store wrap themselves into presents.
It is not willed, it is not me. It is time.

David Head

Playback

"An old record" you said
and, another day,
"Where does the pain come from?"

One setting – a close wood
stranger's hands
my neck and groin.

This time a clinic
two fingers suddenly on pubic pulse
"Oh hell!" Resuscitation.
"Did anybody know she was allergic?"
Panic questions, explanations,
unseen racing figures, "Fetch him now!"
While here inside the body
which excites such sudden interest
tranquillity profound till,
unprovoked, all by itself,
my chest rises in enormous sigh.
"She's respirating!"

No champagne or rejoicing.
All too scared and cross.
"Someone should be told,
letters written, columns in the Press.
Why, if she'd died..."
Well, then there'd be a song and dance.

But I survived and, with no greeting,
this new birth, quite like the last one,
just feels foolish and a little bleak.

Hilary Elfick

Gathering oysters with Eva

(Eva was a Hungarian refugee in 1956,
and now lives alone at Te Wahapu.)

Cutting clusters of oysters from the castles they have built
blood runs between our fingers.
She hits the smallest gap with the point of her knife,
peering closely, bucket balanced on a rock beside her.
"I don't want the ones that are dead."

We carry them up the shell path to the bark door,
rinse them in bore water, leave them to soak.
When the table is ready with new-baked rewana
she drops the bladed chunks in a boiling cauldron.
Waits. Lifts one in a draining spoon
to let it clatter on my plate.
Each hides eight, a dozen, every oyster in its housing.
Crunch them apart, dip them in sour cream,
slide between fingers onto our tongues.

She likes pipi too, and mussels,
but you must dig for those and now the tide's too high.
And crayfish? Does she have a friend who dives here?
She shudders, shrinks, and I'm surprised.
"It is the smell. I cannot stand the smell.
It is like the bodies of the dead in the forest
in the Spring thaw."

Rewana – round potato bread

Hilary Elfick

34

Silent pictures

On edge of bed a woman weeps
Deep in the cupboard rises bread
Round its face the hour hand creeps
Memories slide inside her head

Under a moon about to wane
The iron gate's curling into rust
A raindrop rolls down the windowpane
Dew stills softly into frost

A dragonfly drops to the garden pool
Blade stares in the fallen tarot card
The cold birch leaves have turned to gold
She reads the meaning where there's no word

Curled into cot child sucks his thumb
Koi carp smooch under fallen leaf
The cat walks through the grass alone
A waking lawyer scans his brief.

Hilary Elfick

Beforehand

Good Queen Bess
stands in the window at Sheen Palace
sucking her thumb.
She has stood here for nearly three days
and soon she will fall down dead.
The pain gnaws at her like a Spartan fox.

Move fifteen miles, four centuries.

You with your dried skin and auburn hair
laboriously wield an arm as thin as a sceptre.
Your eyes are closed like a laid-down doll's.
Your lips grip slowly at the moisture
on the pink sponge you poke
at the corner of your mouth.

David Head

This scar

This	scar
cuts	a
straight	weld
down	your
pink	cheek
grown	fat
with	death.
Pale	sides,
raised	skin.
I	see
for	the
first	time
you	are
dy	ing.
It	is
that	thin.
I	can't
ask	when
why	how
your	face
was	marked
as	your
life	drains.
Your	past,
your	life.
I	guess:
at	sport
or	work.
I	want
to	ask
your	wife
and	your
wi	dow
says	you
tripped	in
a	plane.

David Head

Remote control

Atrophy has bent your left wrist at an eighty degree angle,
twisted and locked your knuckles, so your ring finger
lies close to your life line, pointing in at the space
between your loose-hanging watch and your inexorable pulse.

Hello. You put down the remote control on the pink blanket at once
and I hold the thin right hand with hairs like escaping wires
that you reach across your body, then remove the headphones,
with your permission, from your reddened ears.

Your speech is faint and slow, deliberate not slurred,
half-swallowed by the stiff lip of your disease.
I see you speak also with the steadiness of your eyes,
claim the time needed to comprehend, communicate.

Till goodbye. I replace the headphones, slip into your hand
the sleek black remote control, where your right index
repeatedly taps the green "Off" button without vigour or intent,
jerking to the time of your infinitesimally advancing illness.

I would like to change the channel we are on, touch a number
to rearrange life. My hand as free-moving as a sea-anemone
ripples to blur the moment of my walking away. Involuntarily
your arm wobbles with its burden, slightly, like a wave from royalty.

David Head

Haiku

One-time acrobat,
lady, eighty-five, in bed,
struggles to climb out.

David Head

Coming in to land

The window behind is
a column of darkness.

Descending aeroplanes
cross each ninety seconds.

Eighty seconds, then lights.
Eighty seconds, then lights.

Airplanes as images
of repeated decease.

Behind you the crossings
of planes count your losses.

You tell your sadnesses;
all breaks, dies, fails, passes.

Your strongly lighted face
shines with hurt ignorance.

You follow two nurses
with your half-seeing eyes.

Your indistinct voice seeps
into the ward's silence.

In this protective space
you talk yourself to peace.

You continue for hours.
Well, seventy minutes.

I get pins and needles.
I shift along; you pause.

Beyond your hanging words
the dark column changes.

Outside in the darkness
a time-switch lights two globes.

Behind these mimic moons
radiant as your cheeks

another pair of lights,
another plane descends.

David Head

The bullfrog prince

The security-pass photo of a dishy bloke,
handsome thirty, sunset-blond curls,
vibrant eyes dark as the calm night of the soul,
ruler-straight nose, lips toughened with the habit of smiling, competent jaw.
The card's word end marks a place in a book.

I play slow dominoes with the bullfrog prince
in his room beside the wishing well.
Gobs of sun slide on his scarred pate,
his swollen cheeks bag with their burden of blood,
his Victorian stomach only lacks an industrial watch-chain.

I note his football neck as he turns, looks at the willows,
wait for his princess to come through the door, for her lips
to print his face and bring to life the photograph, the fairy tale;
magic away the dimensions steroids have added
and make him the flat hero. Just for a moment. Perhaps.

He hears her doing dishes in the palace, singing to the children,
muttering herself out of the garage in reverse,
the hands that don't often touch him plumping duvets.
The shadows underneath the branches by the pool are cool,
full of irrelevant flies, ants, fish.

He shuts his eyes like she did in the early days when hugging.
Then remembers how she used to, later, in despair,
pull on his lips with hers to kiss the cancer better;
how that dwindled to the odd peck on his crown
when the things in him she'd loved submerged.

She leans against the pillows they shared, stares into the lamp,
sucks the black biro, scribbles in her daughter's pop-up book.
She'll get another one so they won't know.
Gazes through the page and her correction
"And they lived happily ever *until*."

David Head

When you and I

When you and I shall sleep at last
sunk weight, lump, stone
And dusk will fall and mists will spread
damp dust, chilled bone
Then who will watch the Summer pass
sand, sun, sea, shoe
And who prepare the marriage bed?
vows, church, I do

And when the rain has sprung the green
tarn, fall, river, sea
And collared dove held down his mate
oak, ash, podocarp tree
Then who will rake this shingled path
thistle, elder, trowel, trug
And dream of grandchild giving birth
ground sown, earth dug

And when the cuckoo calls at dawn
stole nest, killed kind,
And wakes the roses into bloom
green thorn, dwarfed vine
O who will tell them that we came
hasty, touchy, preoccupied, spent
Discovering most things far too late
wondering where the minutes went

Hilary Elfick

Hospice Uganda
Hoima, 24.10.97

They say that Adam first drew breath in Africa

and certain I have seen his garden hung with mango, coffee, maize,
and watched the stalks of millet bow and curl before the wind.
And through the shades of vast savannah
I have seen the herds and flocks that once he named –
the elephant and vervet, and the shy low squirrel and the porcupine.

I never saw the serpent

but I did see the path where he has wormed
and left his spittle on the puffy cheek of dying child
and scoured away a young girl's fertile time. And here's
a man who hoes his field until he slims with falling sickness   *'slim' = Aids*
quiet into his furrow, and here's a granddad that has lain neglected
these wet months upon a foetid sheet. And there's a maid
whose belly swells with child who will not last his first full year,
and here's a youth whose every knot and tuft of hair
have dropped to show the snake's imprinted skin.

Go forth and multiply? The sap still surges when the sun has fallen.
We say that man acquires his own deficiency;
we call our kind a syndrome.

And we, who make such careless jibes
from our thin quarantine, what can we bring
into these meadows washed with heavy rain,
along these red roads, scarred and pitted
with the blood that runs in Africa?
What pills, what powders, what fine potions can we root
to cover up the dribble of his passing?

Through touch of mist I see this nation's colours stretch
across the sky in bow that pales and leeches into dusk.
In these green blades close by the path I see
the sullen clots that slump and catch the evening light
against a prison hut where this old warder's wife is hunching in her flux,
tongue stiffened in its yellow coat, where hard beams of an equatorial noon
scorched eyes that fleck and flinch and cannot cry.

What parody of Eden's this dark hut
where child, whose mouth swells too grotesque to close,
lies trembling in a pulse that pounds two hundred beats a minute?
What God can we now walk beside at twilight
unless we first have washed him in his fraying blanket caked with waste,
as once again we watch him twist and wait to die?

But this was where first breathed a man.
That is what, at last, will burst the heart.
And still the pineapples are ripening in the fields.

Hilary Elfick

My touch: IV

Once I have touched you, I carry you.
As they slide goodbye, our padded atavistic claws
rasp from one another specks of a being
whose difference is imprinted in every alien double helix.
We implant our coded histories within each other,
sleeping agents of a subversion to which we acquiesce.

Professionalism knows the danger of skin on skin.
I must wash my hands between each patient visit,
perform what nursing books, with the tact of those
who may not be abraded, call "decontamination".
We may not keep each other as forces for change,
host each other, culture or be cultured in exchange.

Until I bath tonight, and put my dirties in the laundry bag
I could house your essence in microcosm on myself,
transferred to the brow I rubbed, hair I clutched,
the cotton sleeve I fretted while I walked away.
I could disregard procedures for the living,
but I want my touch to be benign.

Meanwhile, I do not know how many bodies have been stored
for burial or burning with bits of me attached;
how many final words been spoken over the place
where I, with thousands of others, commingle in the flesh
with someone loved; and where inside the earth
or in the air the ones I've touched have taken me.

David Head

The Hospice Chaplain's Royal Road

I

Ordained to preach a gospel of something
I stand hand in hand with death
this side of an exercise of perspective
where all lines lead to vanishing point.

Before I reached this two-dimensional screen
I used other men's words to paint pictures
of The Royal Road That Leads To Life.

They were coloured
for consolation or forgetting,
and sometimes
with my own ideas for sentiment.

There is a road in this diagram, but it is empty,
stretching away conceptually straight
into the centre of the page.
It is that instantaneous.

II

I am by the way.

III

My function is to ease the passage,
but of whom to what I am not sure.

I play huckstering street-sweeper
flicking imaginary grot from The Golden Highway
between God's heart and another's
to importune both for a half-impatient handout

or speak peace where there is no peace,
spread words as smooth as butter
on the rim of the chute that mirrors this triumphal way
downwards into pretend or endless fire

or call to others from the verge
as their foot swings above the beginning of the paviours.

David Head

Visitor hour

My black plastic strap-snapped watch,
curled inconveniently among keys
in my overloaded pocket, was discarded
for the smooth cube of my alarm.

I tick of clock like a crocodile
creeping up on supine Hooks
embroiled in fighting Never-never-land
for control of their eternal youth.

I face them; square wen stretches cloth over
thigh curved on ward visitor chair
like a secret antique pillbox
clicking out doses of healing time.

Any miracle is way beyond.
Reminders of slow heartbeats,
flannel-muted, acid-edged,
drip on remaining heart-stone.

Longing for tales of derring-do
and treachery, I watch a bedpan
immaterial as a fairy whisked
towards a sluice. Words cover it.

We take talk, dig dark holes in the soul
for light and time to shine through.
Take talk. It is my substitute
for an unbroken watch.

David Head

How to be a Real Chaplain

I'm only tired but it must look like scorn,
to judge from comments or apologies
floating up stairs or along corridors
towards my travelling back.

Look, I've had a hard week, OK? Or I'm busy.
Or manners aren't that important to me
just now. Give me a break. But no.

Each doorway is a gauntlet of bouquets to run,
each corner hides the beggars of emotional baksheesh
with psychic palms outstretched. I have had it to here.
Do I burn out or burn, slum or slip my leash?

This paper, thinner than a pool of pee, receives
the printed shapes that say "piss off".
These I can hide, stood upright in a file.

Like a good anarchist, my confessor is called
"A4". Like Luther's, it's started to say "enough".
Sort your life out – get some sleep or some friends –
change your diet. Silently it tells me

not to use the same rag to wipe the floor
and try to sweep the feelings from my face;
ourselves are so much easier to abuse;

and that once the fluff is in my eyebrows
and the smears of last week's polish on my lips,
I act as if they were my mask, not paint flaking
from those idols, Empathy and Being Available.

David Head

Is it possible to write a "hospice" poem? A response and a question.

Since this is a "hospice" poem, I shall go for overkill.
It will mirror the plethora of pills, smiles and sententious meaning
with convolutions of heartfelt, solemn earnestness.
Though we watch it every day, we have reduced death to an idea.
So I will write down my ideas, and then watch myself do them to death.

I could stop there, but then another patient always comes along.
And another thought, to be battered into acceptance by my loving skill.
I know there are too many full stops, but this is a "hospice" poem.
I come to a full stop, or a pun, when I reach the end of the line.
It is a convenient way of making meaning where there is no meaning.

Another way, of course, is never to end, when I am frightened of
coming to a logical conclusion because I can't see the
logic and everything else seems to make life fuller if I
cram in "the words that count" in the little small wee tiny trivial marginal
space that I've got left which is long enough for a
poem if I write it dense because dense slows down time and
doesn't understand, get understood.

So if you don't really like this poem or any of my "hospice" poems
it's not the point. Where the sharp point has reached is the place where I sit
on the blue stain-resistant ward chairs and am heavy. Which might work if
there were scales on which I jump, and catapulted patients waft up lightly,
as long as I don't, for my own depth of meaning, cosy along the lever in
    empathy.

Perhaps a "hospice" poem is where I put the stuff I'm not allowed to say
or think. Therapy without conjunctions.

But then again... The fault might be in not the feeling but the art,
that cumbersome and boring are correct when dealing with eternal verities,
but you want your poems like salami, tasty but thin enough to see through.
And I don't know, or haven't yet been taught,
how to bring lightness into heaviness without seeming flip or full of holes.

David Head

DEtAcheD

being around

                   those losing their GRIP on life

is   it

any wonder

                                  when

I

                    lose

mi

David Head

The confession

You are supposed to name your sins,
say how often, but your eyes
close round a list of images
and you say simply *sins*
as if God understands.

I am supposed to give you absolution
but your voice rambles on
about what you and God have done
until you feel forgiven
and the moment has gone.

I supposed I had failed;
and then you smiled,
absolved me of my guilt
and made me feel the world
was steady as the hand I held.

David Head

Ten minutes a day

Ten minutes a day
his hands hover over my head.

He taps gently, enters when I yell,
stands like an overgrown schoolboy told he's a lummox.

I have learned to be polite.
He's farouche, skitterish, ready to run
(Jonathan's age, though you wouldn't think it).
The four minutes of conversation, sitting, are a ritual.
I could almost time an egg.

I am tired. When he lumbers towards me
his hanging arms swing like neighbouring pendulums in a clock shop.
He positions himself, looms over me like a gantry.

This is serious; I wait
for whatever it is that warms my head to reach my feet.
I scratch, uncertain if it's a hair tickling
or electric scalp.

Useless childhood clergy drone beyond the curtains
but here we are healing.

Ten minutes a day,
if that kind of time can be measured.
I help how I can.

She clasps my wrist, my fingers.
The wishes in her prayers flow through her eyelids on to my knuckles.
We have been so many people together,
the two of us.

These are for me to be me, for me to be,
as I am content.

Peace finds me.
I shall sleep tonight.

His hands hover over my head.

David Head

Billy is my child

Billy is my child.
He's sixty-eight, I'm forty-three, and I love him.

He lies on his side, his left ear in the pillow, never visible.
His bed smells of his roll-ups.

I feed him industrial ice-cream and raspberry sauce on a fork.
That way you can twist it into his vertical mouth.
It would slip off a spoon.

He was born in a tent.
He was dropped.

I'm lonely, he says.
I'm lonely.

I'm not lonely when there's someone there.

He used to go fishing with a friend.
It's restful, he says.
You look at the birds and the clouds.

His wife died.
When he couldn't go out to work any more, his daughter left home.
He lives by himself.

He's illiterate.
That was because he spent ten years of his childhood in hospital, he says.

He was a woodcarver.
They trained him for that.

I did it properly.
I didn't make as many rejects as other people.
Hardly any.
When you're disabled, you've got to work out the best way.

I feel like I want to mother him.

Thank you, Father, I'm glad that I met you.
It's nicer when you feed me.

I'll come again on Wednesday.

The only way I can look Billy in the eyes is to turn sideways myself.

David Head

Cinquains for a mother and grandmother

We saw
her at the last
fragile and weak
and in her, saw the image of
our births

when our
protection lay
in her strong nurturing.
So, by her bed in that long quiet
vigil

we saw
our strength as her
own frailty's gift. So in
our life and in her fading, merge the
mirrors

so at
the last, we bear
her here as she bore us
through our slow childhood, and we bring
our thanks

our love
our understanding
of that pattern which is
giving and receiving, and which
binds us all.

Hilary Elfick

This woman should have been my mother

This woman should have been my mother.

Sitting here, I see

      framed photographs from home, trophies of her only child
      surrounding her, circled like a Madonna's stars;
      at her feet like the trodden serpent the blankets coil

    lids three-quarters dropped on eyes the blue of fading cornflowers,
      a hand that stayed soft cupped to catch
      the dreams that fall before her wing of white hair

        She should have been my mother

I look at

      thinness of thigh moulding the much laundered sheet,
    emaciated snowkept ridge of gouged glacial Mother Earth
      mounded above the edge of its world, and still

    face turned aside to the always loneliness of being this ill,
      nestle of cotton on reddened cheeks
  slow heave of breath pulling, the tremble of her wedding ring

        She should have been my mother

I look inward

      at my many mothers smiling at inconsequential detail of days,
      the bananas, ferryboats and herons of happenstance,
      the treats and toffees a child knows for metaphors

      she was perfect, perfect husband, house, life, maquillage;
      there was a baby once, pursed pink prune of a face,
      swaddled, screaming, but not for long

you should have been my mother.

Dropping me headfirst into the world was not enough.

David Head

Euphemisms

We hold on to our euphemisms
in small interstices of lesser pain.

The door is closing on this room;
rain has sealed the window fast.

Get-well cards crowd your shrinking space;
fading blossoms toll your hours.

I watch the trembling in your wasted muscles,
trace its nerve ends in my smaller bones

nursing my guilt in hope of absolution.

White lies fill the gaps between our teeth.

Hilary Elfick

Data Protection Act 2002

I dissemble.
I disassemble you,
remove all semblance of you
to illustrate a professional point;
make you emblematic but untrue.

But when I write a case study about you
I'd prefer the whole of you in my picture,
the stain of raspberries on your nightdress,
the practised twinkle at the corner of your eye,
the twisted curl of your thickened toenail,
the 'People's Friend' left open at a recipe,
your sweating son with tattooed knuckles,
your cough that sounds like the flare of a match,
the photo of your husband on your wedding day,
the skin of your left arm stretched and bulbous as a haggis.

I want to document exactly you,
but am reduced by the rules
to telling lies.
You deserve that I record your whole delightfulness,
indicate beyond peradventure
this woman, this one, really you,
joking in the face of death despite
the reason I'm allowed to mention you at all.

David Head

The people who walked in darkness

Digital photograph of blossom,
the blue March sky lending itself
to jigsaw-puzzle schmalz
and redeeming squat buildings.

Even in the strong sun
outside the new patient's room
the visitors' faces waiting for something to finish
are too small to interpret, but separate
as petals caught in the act of falling.

Clicked to magnify five times
they simply blur, as if
descending faster, twisting, blown.

The visitors
looked steadily across the grass
at the cameraman crouched among the daffodils
to improve the angle, and
were unreadable.

Select, delete,
and sky, tree, bricks, grass, people disappear.

David Head

Field of hope

Nothing on the radio feels right.
Politics unpersuasive.
Music wrongly pitched.
And made-up stories only fill an hour

much emptier than mine.
That van's belching muck straight into my grille.
They should keep that hedge trimmed back
if that's the place they have to put the sign.

That. That. That.
Cat. Who's feeding his cat?
Must take a break. Tiredness stiffens.

A roundabout. A Little Chef.
And swathes of dying daffodils.
Fields of Hope.

Hilary Elfick

Before the drive home

Deep blue overhead, shading down
through infinite smooth changes to a rim
of lemon green behind the wood.
Cloudless winter sunset.

Beside the car-park a hundred-year-old oak,
stark, black, flat tone slapped against the glowing sky,
glides its two dimensions to new shapes:
pavement tuts beneath my heels.

Remove my mitten, find the key.
Look up, along, see the trail of deep pink fluff
some high-flown aeroplane has farted out
in a continuous, broadening, thinning stream

redeemed, being precisely there, by catching fire
and crimson, swiped on opposite cerulean.
Cold falls upon my face. All growing things
below seem solid, dull, industrial.

I thunk the automatic locks, look up again.
Inside the feathered wash a point of light
pulls an intense fine line of, now, magenta,
stretches it along the selfsame westward track.

David Head

hair

as you sit in bed your head lolls forward
your neck weak as when new-born

short hair, growing back, spirals a crop-circle from your crown,
delicate, whirling, idiosyncratic as a thumbprint

you point your fontanelles at me,
but you are adult and dying

so no one cups your nape to take the strain,
no broad or yielding shoulder bears the weight

in the tousled patterns pushed first into this world
I read predictions of the life to come, written in radiating growth

once in a healing moment, when my hands buzzed above your
    skull,
I watched the lift of longer hair above your forehead

spiked with sweat into curving thorns

David Head

Your ribcage

The surface of the land, the sea,
ripples like the ribs in your breast.
Your heart pounds away like fifteen men
beneath your dead man's chest.

Your skin lies in thin swathed folds
puckered like the swagged silky mesh
of a translucent wing of cooked skate,
where your breast has lost its flesh.

The centre of your chest is ridges
and furrows, pitted and smooth,
like Passchendaele grass covering
shreds of heroes of your youth.

Between your pyjama top's green stripes,
on your open breast and heart half-hid
your sternum and radiating ribs
clamp like a small determined squid.

Here is your measured centre. Round it swim
your face, yawing, anxious, fearful, and good,
your fretting hands, your cold feet.
Yes, I say, you did everything you could.

Words falter. Your little shell-like
ribcage cannot hear, nor be reassured.
Listen. The love you gave and play down
was heroic. Why else were you adored.

Your ruched eyelids are so anxious,
unwanted tears well and slide.
Nearer, I see covered bone, like nursery bars
keeping some child safe inside.

Do not fear. Dying, your heart will emerge
like a dolphin leaping through waves,
like a child released from night-time shadows,
or heroes from their graves.

David Head

The truth

A green woodpecker, bright as a court jester,
parti-coloured magpies and a sullen crow
have scared the tits and wagtails from this acre lawn,
bob, strut, pierce the earth, flap a yard or two.
The trees beyond are no shelter now,
but the breeding ground of the enemy.

The nurses tell me you can still hear.
Nothing I want to say is repeatable in this busy ward.

I look across your waiting body at the birds.

David Head

Tubular feeding

We said no to that,
watching her tug out
drips that she could reach.

Her skull had bled inside.
The bruising's almost gone
but now she doesn't say anything at all

and her eyes don't seem to focus.
Is her hearing aid set right?
How can you tell if she can't indicate?

And that was them just now
calling from the Ward.
There's a bug that they can't trace

and so all visiting is stopped.
The hospital is full
and someone wants her bed.

A nursing home. These brochures here.
They have a waiting list
that will outlive us both.

I'm standing in her upstairs study
tidying her papers.
We're all too old.

But then again I should just say
the field outside is full of daffodils
against a blue sky and I feel the sun.

There's a lot to make you thankful.

Hilary Elfick

Instructions for my funeral

Get me right, I've gone. It's not me in that coffin
on a journey to heaven with a shroud to take off in.
It's not me because I never was present enough.
I was only ever in bits when I thought it was love.

I was never a hero, nor saint; most of us aren't.
I watched my promise wither like an unwatered plant.
I just lived life till it went, encumbered by worry,
preferring that to ambition, judgement by others, and hurry.

Take care to leave most of me out, please.
I was embarrassing to myself, seldom at ease,
unhappy with compliments, sour with the truth,
hopeless in old age and vacantly arrogant in youth.

And don't tidy me up. I was a person of loose ends.
It's usual to be different people with different friends,
to have separate experiences, ways of speaking and relating.
Don't box me into artificially equal lengths for cremating.

Use the rolling pavement of the church service
to sweep me away undifferentiated. I'd prefer this.
Just make the necessary twenty-three minutes sonorous;
but empty. We wasted dead want no one to honour us.

David Head

Not next of kin

Cast on. Madame Defarge sitting large as a Seine barge
wood-armed ward chair gripping hips sat static
emphatically knitting complex patterns spitting
lancing looks above scooped hooked loops
turning one dimension into two at another blue-
shoed nurse setting her not-next-of-kin straighter
giving a black-handed professional pillow-pat so
his head can roll to see not see see her freed
needle seek the tight furry gap split the cling of
wool on wood blunt front piercing forcing the
fibres apart as shaft caresses shaft seeding
counted revolutions points the finger each thrust
twist rough rasp of yarn sliding on index
lengthens her list of accusations knots links
chains of evidence against the God entangled in
aristocratic tapestries she'd guillotine for death
disease despair and sons measures the length left
with her slicing glance folds her work lips mind
pulls from the sagged bag a wool ball her *ci-
devant* baby's head's soft size and slams her
instruments through its unresisting open eyes.
Cast off.

David Head

Your father phoned

Warm, drowsy in the white gown,
lifted like a child from bed to trolley,
anticipating loss in deepest sleep

and waking fuddled, sore
to a world shrunk to my own shape,
anxiety met by placing of a bolster.

And every time, in time, the quiet nurse,
hand on my arm, "Your father phoned.
We told him you were fine. He sent his love."

A student first, frozen by unfamiliarity
on linen drawsheet tightly stretched
over humiliating rubber mattress,
scared by steel, tubes and procedure,
alienated by the sounds and smells;

and always when those instruments of healing
became distressingly familiar,
new places, wards and tumours,
a circus troupe of changing lacy caps,
new shades of blue about my bed
and all the faces younger,
still that message, tightening my throat.

And now, in unexpected early summer
when robins, fighting for their space
sing and glow with brilliance to match the tulips
it is you who lie there, I who telephone,
sending you my love.

And only now I realise
how one small call compresses all our love
leaving unsaid innumerable moments
of waiting by that still device,
of waiting for the time to call
and dreading to be called.

I had not known
the other end of that short call
had felt like this.

Hilary Elfick

How it was

He was breathing softly, on his side,
pale withered cheek slumping towards his nose,
light bouncing off his ear.
You bent over him, doing something,
doleful, watchful, tender.

I spoke; you straightened.
Beyond your shoulder was my first ever kingfisher,
still in the sunlight. Involuntarily,
"Oh, a kingfisher!" You turned, saw,
and turned back to me, radiant.

He sat in his outrageous turquoise, cream and orange
on the moulded wing feathers of a grey plastic heron.
Along the top rail of the decking a white dove rushed, left to right.
Transversely, below, a near-black moorhen poked.
An eighteen-inch goldfish murked like a challenge in the green water.

You hurried to the next bed. "Look!"
The mother, son, who'd been there overnight
uncurled from their contemplation of the blankets,
scraped their chairs round, bodies animated,
smiles broad as yours, as pointed as the kingfisher's beak.

The bird eyed the slinking carp, the moat,
hunting, then axed into the water, surfaced,
a minnow in its beak, flew up again and crouched,
waving its head to get a better purchase, then bashed
the minnow's skull repeatedly against its perch.

I winced across the bed at violent death.
You watched it flap its head from side to side,
bash this way that way, try to swallow, bash again;
turned, glowing, forgiving nature when you said:
"How lovely to see him doing precisely what he ought."

David Head

Breaking the thread

Is this the last line I can write that you can read?
for still your days go drifting long and slow
your voice has weakened as you lie in bed

against the rasping sheets they turn your bones
it's months since all we had to say was said
and still your days go drifting long and slow

we long to ease the breaking of the thread
the words I try to form you already know
you read them smiling, see me in your head

the loving that we have will never go
nothing now can change when life has fled
and still your days go drifting long and slow

I visualise you turning in your bed
the words I try to form you already know
it's months since all we had to say was said

we long to ease the breaking of the thread

Hilary Elfick

The maypole

you rest beneath a blanket of flowers
knitted petal by petal and stitched into a garden of squares

above the almost stillness of your body
you have set up the ribboned maypole of your soul
and dropped the lilac threads of life into your children's hands

you hold your self high so long
we wonder is it planned

       they tread the come and go
       weaving open baskets with rasping silk on silk
       faint as your sigh
       or wrap the column with an energetic spiral

you centre their dance
on a plane of seeing each other

has a purring dove been pinioning the love-knots
that bind you to the measure

or do you hover
seeing from perpendicular height
into the surface on which we move

       our growing vision of such a covering
       these bands can weave
       when released they flutter down

like an arctic tern fishing off Stornoway
gauging the given time
to fold the air out of its wings plummet
and pierce the iron-grey shifting sea

David Head

Keeping time

The oil I have thumbed across your forehead
catches the light. You face aside,
your distended eye half-hidden in the pillow.
Your breathing lifts and settles your head,
for now, as regular and intermittent
as a lighthouse.

We sit in moments of quietness
marked by your breaths, slower than a bass drum
or the tolling of a bell. The faster rhythm of your heart
broadcasts through the bumping folds
of your black pyjamas.

Your daughter topples slowly, merges her hair
with yours, straight-backed, clinging.
Her sobs keep different time from the shuddering air
pulled into your body.

She sits back. Beneath your jaw, one thick tear-track
follows the line of tell-tale vein and lights up,
glistens with each pulse.

Dwindling light beats in your neck. She sees, and with a tissue
Dabs it dry.

In four minutes you will die imperceptibly.

David Head

Go forth, good Christian soul

The night you went
and your sore shell, leaving the morphine
grew quiet and still

such a storm blew outside
that we remembered the hurricane
two years ago this week
shattering even toughened glass
and spoiling the long-tended garden

yet your stillness
isn't the contrast I expected
nor can I quite see the ravaged places
where Pam and Andrew and Penny
used to watch you kneel
and weed and plant and grow

all I can feel today is
your warm whiskered cheek
rough on mine as you gave your bear-hug
and *"How's Hilary?"*
that I hear today through all this gale
and, hearing, smile

They tell me grief will come and I shall find
the cold wide places where you used to stand
but now, today, I cannot weep
but only feel my soul stretched wide
and breaking into laughter as

"Looks like fun" I hear you say.

Hilary Elfick

Parting

You went away
my rare friend
with my blessing
as you always will

and it takes nothing
from that blessing
that when you had gone
I went in your room

picked up your pillow
and held it close
a few long moments
to my face

Hilary Elfick

A background ministry

Closer to you, turned in, the mother stands,
hands hanging. Her upper arms have become grab-rails
to the ten-year-old on tiptoe pulling herself up
for the chiaroscuro of a daughter's kiss.

The greying effect of distance has touched the corpse,
on whom the dead-room sheets rise and flow,
swill over his form, slide and drop over the bed's sharp edge
like sea tumbling over the rim of a world we have left behind.

I am not really there. I have kept to the background
and touch mother, child, and the dead one's pillow.
I am the pale space upon which walks
the light-filled shadow of a man.

David Head

In the viewing room

For now and ever, your body is still.
Line-lost forehead: all surfaces waxed flat.
Dreamed-out eyes: one almost, one two-thirds shut.
Fine-cut lips: curved to a pale yellow smile.
Strong chin: sharpened by your jowl's backward pull.
Shoulders squared: arms straight: wide band of white sheet.
Mounded huge stomach: lesser hump of foot.
Laundered covers smooth them out: immobile.

...at your unclothed throat the spearhead of skin
wriggles with filigree worms of grey hair
still growing unnoticed, labyrinthine
tracers of one more life's uncoiling spring,
or first thin plumes of smoke before the fire,
or captive soul's first trembling climb in air...

David Head

The visitor sofas

First time: electric doors breathe closed behind you;
the spotlit receptionist rings the ward nurse
and indicates the waiting sofas squared off
by the window;   preoccupied with someone
else, and diffident and strange, you float across,
unwary, are swallowed down. Last time: *en masse*,
you crowd the weakest to the   unsupported
middle seats, as if warmth wards off past events;
banished and obvious, you are sauntered past;
dispossessed, by the dead's remove, of the right
to go unannounced   where you saw them alive.

David Head

Surprised by grief

(to my mother)

1

It was not your fault you were so short
that even I outgrew you, leaving you
nonplussed like a dog in kennels.

In your last weeks your broad body shrank
as you had always wanted, and your lap
and arms grew to include and enfold me
till the sudden bloating of the final hours

and that is how I touched your arm through
all the apparatus and ached goodbye.

2

Contradictions always. Never predictable
yet the clothes you chose so carefully
made you seem so ordinary.
You mended them in thread that never matched.

Your sudden rages scared more than you meant
and your slow justifications clogged and bewildered
my embarrassed puberty. You always tried

your heavy hardest to meet my last year's craving
and now that laboured loving wreaks havoc
with my hunger, worse now than before.

3

That week you lay in Maelor *("your mother's doing*
very well – I'll tell her that you phoned")
I played Lloyd Webber's Requiem full volume in my car
to accompany your dying while dangerous tears
streamed down my face

                     leaving my final vigil
quiet and calm, supportive of my father.
Somewhere that last weekend I lost the tape.

4

When did you ever invite my anger?
You spent restless hours just doing your best.
Who made you the target of my frustrations,
you who would have given all earth's
embroidered colours to lay upon my bed?
Above all it is not your fault that what I feel now is
a rage of grief, accusing you of loss that now seems life-long.

5

Where did our minds miss?
The only route you knew to your many certificates
was so painstaking techniques got in the way
and I never told you how I would have clawed my way home
to your blackout Chopin, played from your heart beneath my room.

When we meet again let me creep, small, behind you in silence
while all your words in which I floundered and drowned
lie unheeded at your feet, and, seated at the piano you left me
play me all twenty-four of those lost *Preludes.*
To them I could awake finally with love.

Hilary Elfick

Attention

One only wreath of flowers, white, restrained, silent trumpets
perpendicularly above your heart encased in the mortal flesh it collected,
that in turn encased in chipboard, oak veneer, and those handles that fool no
    one.

Mutes with loose dark shoulder-pads lower you, your head towards the altar,
to the trestles, with that soft scraping rasp like the slip of a shoe on parquet
when a body crumples, hits the corner of a desk and jerks to the floor.

The coffin's hidden by the crowd, the overcoats and suits of closer people,
front row family and early comers, those who loved enough
to take a whole day's holiday and come to this homely, sodden countryside.

The hymns are chosen to be known, but sung like bicycling in fog;
we're tentative, miserly with the breath that remains to us, do not want to
    sound
operatic, or rich, or self-obsessed, or cheerful, or too alive.

Beneath the dog-tooth Norman arches the bishop climbs into the pulpit,
begins a eulogy that remembers God through the lens of your life, says
    "attention"
was the watchword of your ministry, your prayer, your time, your love.

I drink in new stories of your mimicry; relax my shoulders, smile at
    reminders –
to me as well you said: "Prayer is absolute attention to what is the case."
To all these others too, no doubt, and they no less loved for being many.

Your face assembles in my mind's eye that will not cry, mobile maybe
because I have no photograph of you to slowly tie it down, can not reduce
our hours together to a lamina, your humility to a pose.

With a lurch of loss for a moment that cannot be recaptured,
for information unheard and unstored, I return. For the last ten seconds,
I realise, I have been thinking about yesterday's TV.

David Head

Letting go

Under a grey and winter sky
my car sweeps this wet winding road
across the half-tamed moors.
Three women buttoned closely at a bus stop,
two heads above dark collars in the car in front,
I read them all as going to the gathering in the church upon the hill.
Just so my thoughts have narrowed or the world itself has widened
to this last, reluctant parting.

The church is white with flowers, drapes and candles,
dressed as for a bride. I never saw your wedding,
but as the incense swings like orange blossomed spray,
her acolytes like bridesmaids, I feel this second marriage
making tribute to the first, a practice run for now,
the marriage that begins, not ends, with death.
And so these people whom I do not know
draw back that fine white veil to show the shining brown beneath
and place the wreath, a wiser coronet, upon the wood.

Her father handed her to you that day (when I was still a child),
and now, he long since gone ahead, you stand close by
to hand her to the Bridegroom. Up on the higher altar
I see one candle waver, splutter, shrink and then stand empty,
bleak among its fellows. You turn to go
(my face like windscreen trickling in the rain)
pull on your coat, and bury deep your empty hands.
But in that old forgotten pocket are the neat stitched gloves
she made you, still a maid, not yet your bride.
You handle them, an icon, telling me they always were
a mite too small, and that is how they've lasted.

But so it was and always is
for what we stitch and weave with love
is always smaller than the love itself,
our hands too big and clumsy for the gift.
The icon, lasting, fits inside a pocket,
talisman against a colder cold than winter
where the wild white sky, the waking morning
and the crossword, only ever now half-finished,
speak the silence of an unlit flame.

Only remember this, remember this
that when you'd left the church and marriage bed
we stood there with those other candles burning, burning,
guarding yet those little lights to warm your folded hands.

Hilary Elfick

After the wake

It is the details that you don't expect.

Saucepans heavy, full, lids so sealed
with grease or some mysterious vacuum
that first I cannot prise them off, and then
I do not want to.
                              Small jars of greying dust,
priced one-and-six on sticky faded labels.
Flour bags dot with weevils animated
like the squirrels this bright morning on her grave.
Scratched tin that might still guard a fruitcake marks
a coronation with a portrait – George the Sixth.

Stacks of china, earthenware.
Discard the chipped and cracked
and all the orphaned saucers, wash the rest,
stacking them in remnants of lost tribes –
yet here's the Limoges sugar bowl
she kept for best and quite forgot, and look
how still the apple-blossom gleams as once
her eyes before the smudge of frailty.

And now to fill the sink again, to scour
and cleanse, scrub shelves, and kneel upon the grit
of spilt rice grains, date-marked from that first stroke
whose ringing marked her Compline.

She had him build this larder close to
her proud range, so pretty then with jars of
fresh-dried parsley, mint and chive,
and all the Christmas reds of strawberry compote,
brewed in this great pan I now use for a skip.

"I used to buy her biscuits in bright tins,"
Stan said, *"so she could use them for her parkin.*
They marked events, like trips to foreign parts,
a special birthday, Easter or a crowning."

Hilary Elfick

Talking with Sarah

But Mum, why not move house? Redundant rooms,
unweeded beds and lawns so wide for mowing?

          O love,
in finding space to filter
all the fruitful from the grinding
now that we've passed through thirty years
of frail, uneasy coupling

we're trying to retrace those steps
where souls pricked out on careless knives
forgotten toys and scribbled notes
and mopped up spills and muddling

                              so must we now make time
to bring those tentatively bought bright chairs,
those added beds and tables, rehemmed drapes,
here out in front to sag and fade beneath a staring sun,
a *worth resuscitation?* tag just dangling in the breeze

dismantling dreams where hammered fingers bled
and milk boiled over on the cluttered stove
and games kits turned and tangled
through The Round (and steamed up) Window

lift down from attic dusty, talcumed, cradle
whose stale and tugging sweetness cuts more deep
than willow, slow unweaving round its ribbons,

expose before you all our clumsy errors
faster than our wondering hands can handle
so we are tidied into boxes you and we can bear?

Not yet then? Must it be, and always be,
and always be tomorrow?

                              O love,
        Time. Time besieged, besieges us.
        We think and move against it.
        It's never time.

Hilary Elfick

Truth

Body equals memory bank.
Can't deceive.
Tells what I ate
how much I drank
won't cover for me

sneaks on me when I'm winded
stumbling up the hill
clumsily last

scar by my ankle
twinges instant recall
of crutches and frustration

awkward movement
reminds me precisely
where I fell
twenty years gone now

and when you touch me, here,
I taste the hands that bruised me

and when you hug me
you, my mother's height,
I cannot hold the tears.

Hilary Elfick

Esther

Grieving my missing daughter
I turned and found you there
Ready to bake a cake.
"You look sad today" you said
Comfortably kissing me
"I like it here."

By what miracle did you come today
My other, borrowed, daughter
Freeing me to be a mother
The day I lost my child?

Hilary Elfick

One room

One room for cooking
Five rooms for sleep
Two rooms for dining
But no room to weep

Three rooms for sitting
With lamps to read by
Two rooms for bathing
But no room to cry

A garden for sunning
With poolside and bar
But no room for sobbing –
You sob in the car

Three rooms for sitting
Five rooms for sleep
A garden for sunning
But no room to weep

Hilary Elfick

Winter

Winter mists obliterate the skyline.
Stillness in the laden trees.
Ice-fast ground.
Deep quiet of snow.

Bone-cold, the wild rabbit
Crouches between the railway sleepers.
Cat, bewildered, picks his way
Seeking his clump of heather
To relieve himself. Stands listening
Confused by cold.

Not a postcard sky
Grey, brooding,
No longer reflected in the hard pool.
White marks below the ice
Show where the carp died,
Embedded now in the thickening slab.

Winter and despair show the same arrogance,
Claiming the last word.
Where no poems are left
One anachronistic spear of green
Has cheeked its way through the shroud.

Hilary Elfick

David Shand

So wide is the space
that he left her
and so loud the rain

who ever would have thought
that all the wreaths
for his six whole days
would have been so very small?

Hilary Elfick

Grief through the kitchen window

Ah. So "Nature abhors a vacuum".
I must be Nature. Upstairs, the bedroom
gapes.

My oak trees outside in the next garden
hold up branches for my frost to harden
grey.

My blear-eyed sky grimes the space above earth
with air even my magpies don't find worth
while.

My shrubs hug the suburban wooden fence
uneven-sized, even-spaced in a dense
rank.

My brown leaves heap beneath plants to decay
or breed my blackbirds meals of workaday
bugs.

My milky sun with its low winter slant
hides from the spiky frozen lawn it can't
clear.

My cold running water for the kettle
swirls round deposits on its curved metal
bones.

The world-wide savour of uncurling tea
smells of – only me, only me, only me.

David Head

What I meant

Don't talk to me
when I'm curled up crying.
Don't ever ask me
to try and explain.

Don't examine me
when I seem lonely
or look for logic
in my pain.

The only way
you'll reach my sadness
is hold me closely
– just now and again.

Hilary Elfick

In grief

If your hand ever, ever, ever
Were to take flesh once more,
I'd lightly touch the surface of your skin with one finger over and over
And sense every pore.

If your eye would ever open
To be clear and soft and see,
I'd look in and in into the blackness where all things happen
Beyond reflections of me.

If your mouth were ever mobile –
Spoke, laughed, admonished, kissed –
I'd watch a thousand moving ways of welcoming different people
Which no longer exist.

If your heart were ever pumping
Life again through your gone veins
I would put my ear to your chest and count each second that something
Physical remains.

If your breath were ever flowing
Out and in and out and in
I'd feel the coolness on my cheek and tell myself everything was always
      going
To be as it had been.

David Head

The mortal coil

The coin fell, clunked inside the machinery,
and a bulb two inches high, shaped like a flame,
began to flicker, among the others on the rack.

The church that surrounded me was black-walled
with the smoke and gutterings of ancient candles,
and smelt of damp stone, silence and prayer.

I'd come to celebrate the glories of your life in fire,
only to be fobbed off with this ersatz lightning,
less, even, than imitation of the electricity between us.

I wanted a candle, a living light to glow, content,
with the steadiness of your sleeping breath.

I wanted a symbol of you, envisaging something
self-contained, individual, lambent, with its own beginning and end,
lit by a spark, not meretriciously turned on by money.

It should have been something fleeting, for you are gone.
I cannot switch you on and off; we do not have a measured, equal time
to live; we do not just go out, we are consumed.

Then, like a crematorium rosebush uprooted when its lease is spent,
a light beside the one I lit for you goes dark, and I repent.
Flicker, little filament, be brave, keep going. Any light on memory will do.

David Head

Coming out of the casket

A polished container, not of your choosing

In which heap your ashes, darked from the world.

Great grey grief, powdery grains, ground bone.

I would choose you a nestling resting bosom of earth;

Loving, leafy light; dappled warmth; forgetful, tumbling water,

A single spring bubbling meanings and mysteries.

Other hands would pass your helpless box around, measure out

Small dollops of dust and ashes they hope mean repentance –

Watching their control of you leaving, not where you land.

David Head

The Black Falls

After he died, I came back to the falls
hoping they'd play proxy for my tears,
but light mist, blowing in the afternoon sun,
shows me only the fall of his grey hair
over his generous face, honed shining to washed stone.

Cowslip and campion, elderflower, sage,
crowsfoot, laburnum, grasses and birch,
soft shy leaf of the new-born holly,
rowan branches, softly blown
cluster, mingle, either side his flowing bed.

Before it falls, the river pauses,
slips the edge, then plunges down
falling headlong into turbulence
of foaming bubbles, slips sideways
across the eddies, boulder-sliding,
and in the tumbling spurts, his breathing
struggles, rasps, percolating,
while, like birch root, I cling exposed,
waiting, crouched and helpless. Wait.

When that sound went, his last awareness
lingered lightly in the silence.
Leaning on his bed, I stood
and stroked and stroked and stroked the hair
which, damp, lay spread on that pared flesh.

"He was a good age when he died"
one said, as if the catastrophic
loud obliteration of these rocks
might somehow be quite sensibly forgiven
because, of course, we'd had our worth of them.

In this small patch, where sun caresses,
wounds creep out most carefully,
larkspur, rose hip, cowslip, campion,
below the rumble of the falls
which still, betraying, loose no tears
but only the hard ache of his dying,
while still the grey mist softens outline
and still the silver strands fall
over rock so like a human face.

Hilary Elfick

Linn

stands still a moment, watching.
Uncovering mud, steel blue, plips and splats.
The black dog stops too, waits.
His cap, a heron's beak, is carved still,
then moves fractionally and is moveless again,
part of him. His eyes drink.

The marsh he played on as a school-age child
given up to a death that waited;
the banks that hid him, his gun, his dog in half-light;
tendrils of seawater combing in and out between the sea-lavender
each tide; the birds.
The luminous flatness.

Dropping sun whitens the blinding water.

Plodding on, they team, he seeing in his mind
the lawn he's come from, deck-chairs, tea,
the shrubs he planned, the creeper-covered house,
her masculine hands, the stem of smoke.
A west wind brushes grass stalks on his calves.

Hears laughter and the golden boy is back
learning birdsong, shooting, flowers, ideals;
with his own intelligence, love, gravity, awful jokes.
We came this way so many times, you were like the
September swallows catching all manner of thing
high or sweeping wide or skimming the bank before my feet.

The ten-year ache. His drowned so-nearly son.

They reach the dunes. Soon it will be water's edge, then sea.

David Head

Papa Westray

The lane sunk into the soft spine of the island,
cattle not yet mustered lean over the hedge
to watch me leave.

In the shade of the long slow wall of the church
my footsteps put up a soft echo.
Inside, the columns have stolen cobalt and scarlet
from the chequered glass
and the lingering afternoon's low shaft
burns the bowls of marigolds.
A place to shed shoes.
My saints lie here inscrutable,
named on walls and under stone.

Outside, toward the shoreline
Magnus Blackcat purrs to meet me,
feels my familiar fingers, licks my thumb,
looks back to where the ebbing tide
strokes the shingle.
A fulmar swings an ovoid path
repeats, repeats, dipping her wing
a fingertip away.

The boat slops by the tiny quay,
motor reluctant. Then fires.
I will myself on board.

The tidal rip and shaft of slowly slipping sun
incise this separation.
A smudge on that wide shore, my black cat watches still.
The fulmar's dropped to the grass tufts
where the tide has fallen.
An evening wind overwhelms, even here,
with sudden scents of cow and ryefield,
drying bladderwrack, sour skin of seal.
I have pulled close under my chin
this scarf where milk cow slavered her green chewing,
and Magnus left his muddy spoor.
I pull inside my head the slices of scarlet, cobalt,
the raised runes of my lost saints
and the wide swathes of the ryefield.

Hilary Elfick

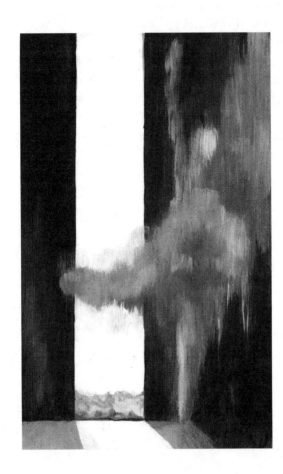

For George Mackay Brown

Salcombe Estuary, 30th May 1996

It's now I miss you most,
      most find you,
      listening here to wind and ripple,
      flap and tug of sailcloth, jerkin,
last blustered day of May and nearing solstice,
the first waymark you will not, waking, see.

A month past Johnsmas
      I was due to sit with you at Mayburn
      in your unpretentious house where
      kitchen served for galley and for skalboard.
      Yet I shall come,
expect to see you still

not under Magnus columns where
      the red stone bled our sudden cleaving,
      nor in that noust above Hoy Sound
      where fulmar dips her wingtip to salute you
but where a cat still curls below your stair.

But now I sit and write between green hills,
      see water-light as through your eyes
      and hear the cry of gull and crow,
      watch scudding puffs of saturated grey
      race low across a cold blue sky
and read of lark and snowflake, candles, kirkyard,

feel, way across the haar that lies between us,
      your hand that eases still my swanway, sharkway,
      and held a candle high against my face,
when you paused a while, perusing, and were glad.

Hilary Elfick

Elegy for a tutor

What is grieving, but attending to the fact that you have gone?
That coffin of abnormal length still settles under chunks of sandstone
while blaze of rhododendron fades above your grave
and distant hills of Wales beyond this grassy slope
still wait to shimmer in a creeping summer.

Alongside your discerning ear my own became attentive.
I learnt to hear and look and taste, forgot how to evade,
slipped off the habits that wrapped truth in palatable words.
Some forty years since first I heard you speak
in those small rooms that lie below us in the valley
and yet I still can hear your voice and crave your measures.
Forty years of friendship. It was Socrates who said
"of all loves, this the best." And Christ, our Brother...

Back home, at this address you often wrote
upon a postcard when you, travelling, thought of me,
one comes up to the door, another phones,
a neighbour wants a favour. I cook a meal.
The news hour comes and goes. Rain falls.

The sun darts out to brush swift strokes between the shadows.
Squirrel takes her little leaps across the stubby lawn.

The cat sits down to preen.

A blackbird *flings*
her lyrics on the pollen-laden air.
O can I make a canticle like hers
to imprint on this time a carol
that will set these leaves a-ringing —
in pace, in amore, in aeternum
cum tuo semper, sum sola
Eleri dilecta?

But I am looking at the grass and sifting words.
I am attending to the fact that you have gone.

Hilary Elfick

Echo

You were a strand in life's music. I sometimes hear
an echo of the melody you were
when the street is silent, the door locks out the night,
and everything within gives off your note
like the clear ringing of cut glass tapped by a knife
singing with its emptiness. Like my life.

I close my eyes to listen, or it sounds so wrong:
the single missing part distorts the song
of everything. I set my mind to recapture
and replay your tune, and often your dear,
strong refrain resumes, and my heart is overwhelmed
with memories of the difference you made.

One day your song began, another it ended;
between was beauty. Death only undid
the power to make more. I seek out those places
where most I sense the history of your voice.
I love to hear your echo in my inner ear
before I too, and my song, disappear.

And if there's more, if truly since the beginning
there has been heavenly music that we sing
with planets, stars and atoms in a stately dance,
taking our part now here, now there; then let's
sing to one another across the unseen space –
and practice for our singing face to face.

David Head

The meeting in the garden

She, supposing him to be the gardener, turned.
Together, like first Adam and first Eve
in the first paradise, the one unearned,
alone, they looked. And she did not believe.

"Where have you put him?" Thus the broken heart,
crying from misery, fear, self-blame.
Hope beyond hope, joy of joy, with a start
she staggered, trembled as he called her name.

Her hand reached, stretched like a lily bursting
into bloom, opening to drink sunshine
from the source that, to her, meant everything;
she made to grab the arm of the divine.

"Don't hold me back, my dear. I may not stay.
The tree has done its work, and you are free.
Go now," she heard the second Adam say,
"and tell the others what you see in me."

David Head

Courtyard at Emmaus

Figs rarely ripen in this garden. Christ knows
that I should now cut down this tree, but while its
wide apocalyptic leaves still give good shade
I shall withhold my axe.   Along these branches
I have hung my baskets   of forget-me-nots,
love-in-a-mist and   silver thyme, and at its
feet I've set my tubs   to trail sweet lavender
and dill and chive.   I sip my wine here and I
crumble bread for sparrow, thrush and turtle dove
and   read a verse and scribble lines; look up to
find my Lord still here across the dappled shade.

Hilary Elfick

After the harvest

You were an unexpected spring
watering my cracked and dusty land,
and, at your touch, astonishing
new flowers broke, quite shyly,
through the thorns and blossomed
into shapes and colours you and I
never could have guessed at from the label.

When a spring fails
the water grows first bitter
and then dry. The flowers
last a while, as if some half-lost
lingering memory keeps moist
their shrinking, hidden channels.
Perhaps your flow is seasonal.
I only know I'm sad to feel
your dryness and to watch
the old cracks open in the ground
and fallen petals curl, pale and forgotten.

And yet I even now hold fast and claim
if even five and twenty seasons come
and go without so rich return of harvest
it was a good, the best, a vintage spring
and worth the scars the thorns left in my hands.

Hilary Elfick

Litany

for Donald Nicholl

my psalm is the sound of one hand clapping
the raven stoops to bring me food
raindrops touch with a single tapping

a laser pierces the hand on the rood
purity of heart is to will one thing
and to will one thing you must will the good

one hand claps like a rook's wing beating
the plainest chant beneath the hood
two hands missed and tumbled flapping

a candle trembles, the flame is blood
the song remains as one toe tapping
all things meet at the point of the rood

my cry is the sound of one hand clapping
the single sound of the hole in the rood
the purest heart only wills one thing
and to will one thing is to will the good

Hilary Elfick

Previously published poems

Meg, Mary, Playback, Surprised by grief, Truth, Esther, One room, Winter, David Shand were all first published in Hilary Elfick's collection *The Horse Might Sing*, published by Envoi 1990.

Iles Lavezzi, Your father phoned, Go forth, good Christian soul, Parting, What I meant, After the harvest were all first published in Hilary Elfick's collection *Unexpected Spring*, published by Envoi 1992.

Questions, Writing out the Angst I and *II, The Black Falls* were all first published in Hilary Elfick's collection *Going Places*, published by Envoi 1994.

Gathering oysters with Eva, Hospice Uganda, Talking with Sarah, George Mackay Brown were all first published in Hilary Elfick's collection *Harpoon the Breeze*, published by Guildford Poetry Press 1999.

Breaking the thread was first published in *New Blackfriars*, July/August 1997.

Litany first appeared in Adrian Hastings' Preface to Donald Nicholl's *The Testing of Hearts*, published by Dartman, Longman, and Todd 1998.

A background ministry was previously published in *The American Academy of Hospice and Palliative Medicine Bulletin*, Summer 2001.